This book is dedicated to my mom an[...] for always supporting me and showing me how to be a great parent.

the Sum.

EMOTIONS
Classroom Posters

How are you feeling?

ADDITION
TABLES 1-9

When Mom cooks her sauce, everyone is a winner.

and thinks that she'll have the pasta *her* way.

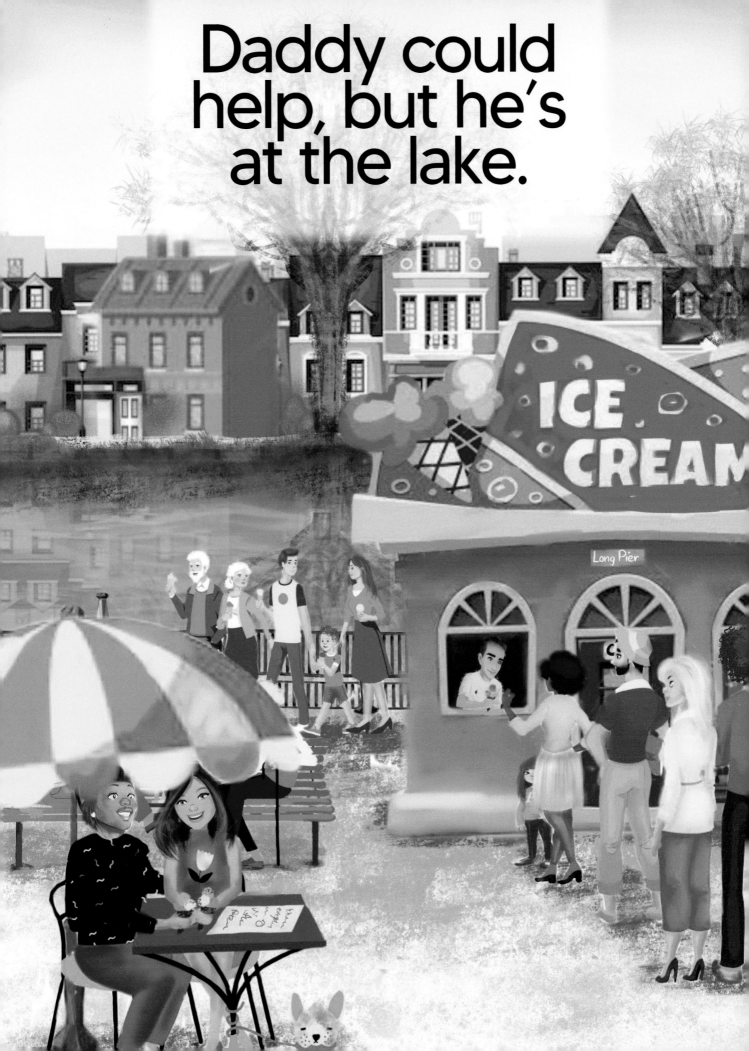

I love rigatoni,
penne, spaghetti,
ravioli, cellentani,
gnocchi,
and cavatelli.

There are so many shapes, and they all are so good.

She's been acting
this way
my whole
childhood.

I peek in the
kitchen as she
sweeps with
the broom.

"Choose the shape
that you want,"
Mom calls out to me.

I know that my sister has chosen rotini.

With a rush of relief, I grab ditalini.

"The best of both worlds," Mom says as she smiles
with the grater in hand, mounding huge, cheesy piles.

Daddy walks in and asks, "How are my girls?" As our cheeks fill with pasta, we brush back our curls.

"You have the very best mommy that ever could be!"